Original title:
Quantum Quips

Copyright © 2025 Creative Arts Management OÜ
All rights reserved.

Author: Amelia Montgomery
ISBN HARDBACK: 978-1-80567-863-2
ISBN PAPERBACK: 978-1-80567-984-4

The Jolly Universe

In the cosmos, stars do giggle,
Planets dance, oh what a wiggle!
Gravity's a jester in disguise,
Holding us close with its funny ties.

Asteroids play tag around the sun,
While comets join in just for fun.
Black holes sing a deep bass tune,
Laughing at light that can't leave soon.

Entropy's Eloquent Anecdotes

Chaos wrote a tale last night,
Of socks that vanish, quite a sight!
Dinner plates dance on their own,
Making mischief in their home.

Time ticks forward, backward too,
Socks have parties when we're not due.
Entropy chuckles, a joke that's sly,
As order crumbles, just wondering why.

Whispers of Uncertainty

Particles giggle, can't decide,
In a dance of chance, they take a ride.
One moment here, the next, gone,
In such a twist, we're turning on.

Certainty's a myth, they say it's true,
Just like that cake that wasn't for you.
With every choice, a laugh shall ring,
In this playful game, what will it bring?

Threads of Entangled Wishes

Wishes tied in a quantum knot,
Shared across space, like an odd plot.
Entangled dreams, they often peek,
At secrets whispered when we speak.

Twisting fates, a funny dance,
Aligned and misaligned by chance.
From one to another, giggles flow,
In a web of wishes, what a show!

Sonnets in Superposition

In this state, I can be two
A pizza slice, or maybe a shoe.
In every choice, I see the fun,
A cat who naps, yet still can run.

In parallel worlds, I like to play,
A juggling clown, or a wise vieux sorcier.
With every laugh, I twist and bend,
Reality's rules? We'll just pretend.

Lighthearted Leaps Through Dimensions

Jump through portals, oh what a sight,
To giggle in the day and dance at night.
Each twist and turn brings joy anew,
Like socks that vanish, oh where are you?

I hopped to Mars for an alien joke,
Their humor's dry, but they're no bloke.
We cracked a laugh and shared a snack,
A cosmic kite flew from my pack.

Vortex of Verses

Spinning words out in a whirl,
Colors clash and dances twirl.
A rhyme can tickle, a pun can tease,
In this wild line, we embrace the breeze.

Round and round, the verses blend,
Who knew a quark could be a friend?
In silly sails, we drift and sway,
Riding the waves of the playful day.

Interstellar Whispers

Stars giggle softly, like old pals,
Whispering secrets, in cosmic halls.
A comet's tail tickles the moon,
While Martians play cards, humming a tune.

Across the void, a voice will chime,
"Why wear a watch? We stretch out time!"
Cosmic humor floats in the air,
With every quip, they're filled with flair.

Waveform Winks

In the realm where particles play,
Light dances with a cheeky sway.
Waveforms giggle, riding the breeze,
Tickling photons, as they please.

Entangled pairs, humor so bright,
Sharing secrets in the night.
Jokes exchanged at the speed of light,
Laughter echoes, a joyful sight.

Quantum Dreams and Cosmic Schemes

In a dream where logic bends,
Stars wink and twist, where nonsense blends.
Thoughts flicker, like fireflies gleam,
Building worlds in a cosmic dream.

Gravity chuckles, pulling tight,
Galaxies whirl in a playful flight.
Logic's adversary, chaos beams,
In the universe of funny schemes.

Collider of Thoughts

At the accelerator of absurdity,
Ideas collide in sheer hilarity.
Fragments of laughter, spinning around,
In a vortex where giggles abound.

Particles pounce, matter and play,
Making sense in a jumbled way.
Bursting with joy, like fission's glow,
Nonsense erupts, and off we go.

Schrödinger's Smile

A box of jokes, both here and there,
One moment serious, the next a flare.
Schrödinger grins, his secrets confined,
In a paradox of the funny kind.

Two states of joy, a laugh that's sly,
Caught in a giggle, oh my, oh my!
Entangled in joy, we can't decide,
Whether the chuckle's on the inside.

Dances of Entangled Destinies

Two particles spin, what a sight,
Twirling in chaos, day and night.
They laugh at gravity, a cosmic jest,
While we fall down, they'll just rest.

In their dance, will we find a clue?
A partner's snicker, an atomic woo.
Steps may be random, but oh so neat,
Their tango of fate cannot be beat.

The Uncertainty Principle of Love

Love's a game of chance, it seems,
Where hearts are wild, not as they gleam.
One moment close, the next apart,
Is it physics, or the human heart?

You look at me, but are you true?
Or just a wave, a bright view?
In love's strange lab, we mix and collide,
Knowing the answer, we still can't decide.

Rhythms of Reality

The universe hums a quirky tune,
Stars throw confetti, the cosmic boon.
Each atom dances in whimsical chatter,
What's real or illusion? Does it matter?

Spin me a tale of a multiverse wide,
With giggling galaxies in cosmic glide.
Reality bends like a silly prank,
Knocking on doors of the absurd, we thank.

The Imprint of Cosmic Imagination

In the cosmic kitchen, ideas stir,
Brewing a brew, a poetic blur.
Thoughts collide, like jelly beans,
Crafting the universe in vivid scenes.

With a wink from the stars, imagination flies,
Creating cats that vanish, oh, what a surprise!
In every quirk and cosmic play,
We spot the humor in the grand ballet.

Particle Whispers

In the realm where particles play,
Little bosons dance in a fray.
Photons giggle, waving hello,
Eager to see where they might go.

Electrons spin with such delight,
In a world that's mostly light.
They tease with tricks, a game of hide,
On a wave, they joyfully ride.

Subatomic Laughter

Neutrons chuckle in a spin,
Protons grin, let the fun begin.
Together they form a tiny jest,
Nucleus giggles, it is the best!

Up and down quarks in their play,
Joking about their funny way.
They frolic, twist, and twirl around,
In this small world, joy is found.

Entangled Echoes

Two particles tied with a wink,
Separated, yet they still think.
One laughs far, another so close,
Sharing jokes like a playful ghost.

In their dance of distant fate,
Comedic chaos they create.
Knocking on each other's door,
With a punchline—who could ask for more?

Theories of Uncertainty

In a world where nothing's clear,
Particles wink, giggle, and cheer.
Uncertainty rules the cosmic show,
But they still find ways to blow.

A cat's alive and then it's not,
Tales like these give quite a plot.
In laughter, truth may find its way,
Though details might be hard to convey.

Celestial Charades

Stars twinkle in a cosmic dance,
Where comets streak with a whimsical glance.
Planets spin like they're caught in a game,
While black holes giggle, who can keep tame?

Galaxies swirl as they hide and seek,
While meteors bark, 'We're unique!'
Asteroids play hopscotch on a wider road,
In this vast playground, imagination's the code.

Enticements from Across the Cosmos

The moon winks, a mischievous tease,
Jupiter jests with his gas-filled breeze.
Saturn's rings giggle, a dazzling display,
While Venus whispers, 'Come dance and play!'

Stars barter wishes, like candy at a fair,
'Wish upon me, if you dare!'
Lightyears away, they share their delight,
In this circus of wonders, a dazzling sight.

Playful Paradoxes of Being

In a universe where time likes to bend,
I met my future self; we became good friends.
'What's the secret?' I asked with glee,
'You're asking me? It's all hazy!'

Matter and energy in a jolly embrace,
Dance like two partners in a bustling space.
Reality's layers peel back with a snap,
In a fabric of fun, there's always a lap.

Dreamweaver of Dimensions

In dreams, I weave fabrics of time,
Each stitch a thought, each knot a rhyme.
I flip through dimensions like a comic book,
Where laughter's a currency, take a look!

Voices echo from realms yet unseen,
Making me chuckle, 'Oh, what a scene!'
Silly adventures unfold with a grin,
In a tapestry where antics begin.

The Dance of Subatomic Dreams

In a world where particles prance,
Electrons spin, they love to dance.
Neutrons giggle, protons play,
Making jokes in a quantum way.

Waves and orbits twist and twirl,
In a universe that's in a whirl.
Each little quark has a tale to tell,
In their tiny realm, all goes well.

They ride on beams of light so bright,
Chasing shadows, never out of sight.
Every collision sparks a laugh,
In their subatomic photograph.

With every bounce a story unfolds,
Of cosmic giggles and playful molds.
In this dance, we all should join,
For in their world, we all can coin.

Particles of Playful Thought

In a cloud of thoughts so light,
Particles ponder left and right.
They tickle the strings of reality,
With a grin that sparks vitality.

A photon winks, a neutron hums,
While gravitons jiggle to the drums.
In this quirky cosmic spree,
Curiosity blooms like a glee.

Ideas collide in joyful bursts,
Each fleeting whim ignites our thirst.
From chaos springs a punchline bright,
In a cosmos of infinite delight.

So let's rejoice in the absurd,
Where silence speaks, and dreams are stirred.
For in this dance of thought so free,
Laughter echoes through eternity.

Relativity in Rhyme

Time travels fast, just like a car,
But who knew space could raise the bar?
With every tick, a joke's on cue,
In the realms where few dare to pursue.

Einstein chuckles from the past,
Saying, "Time's a joke that's unsurpassed!"
With every glance, the world can bend,
A playful twist that has no end.

Between the lines of physics' prose,
Lies a humor nobody knows.
As light beams race and planets sigh,
The universe whispers, "Give it a try!"

For in relativity's embrace,
We find the fun in every place.
In this spiral dance of jest,
We soar through space, we feel so blessed.

Echoes of Particle Poetics

In the hallways of a particle fair,
Tiny beings leap without a care.
Like poets lost in rhythm's grace,
They write their tales in cosmic space.

With every collision, laughter fires,
As they weave through mystical wires.
A photon quips a witty line,
Illuminating the grand design.

In quarks and waves, we find our muse,
Each observation is a playful ruse.
They dance in circles, round and round,
In the silence, see the joy unbound.

So let us join this merry throng,
In the dance of life where we all belong.
For in the echoes of their glee,
We find the truth of what we see.

The Elegant Absurdity of Atoms

Atoms dance in a tiny space,
Waltzing in a comical race.
Electrons giggle, protons tease,
All while fissioning with ease.

Neutrons lounge without a care,
Floating 'round in thin air.
They play tricks with all their charge,
Making physics look quite large.

A quark tells tales of distant lands,
While leptons make the funniest hands.
With every split, reality bends,
Leaving us to laugh, as science sends.

In a world governed by silly rules,
Atoms giggle, as we are fools.
The universe tickles, a grand display,
In this absurd dance, we find our way.

Jests in the Ether

Puppets bob in quantum string,
Every wiggle, a cosmic fling.
They whisper jokes in waves of light,
Tickling stars with pure delight.

A photon winks, 'I'm not what you see,'
He zips around, light as can be.
Opposites attract in a spacetime hug,
Creating chaos, like a snug bug.

Entangled pairs giggle in sync,
What's yours is mine, don't even think!
In a loop that goes around and round,
They prank the universe, unbound.

Such jesters are they, in this grand play,
Making us chuckle throughout the day.
In the ether where nothing's absurd,
Lies laughter that simply must be heard.

Mysteries of the Microscopic

In the tiny realms where oddities dwell,
Subatomic particles weave a spell.
Quirky creatures, in a minuscule race,
Hide in shadows, laughing with grace.

They spin and zoom with delicate flair,
Creating mischief in the smallest square.
With each collision, a silly surprise,
They peek from corners, with twinkling eyes.

Protons strut, like they own the show,
While neutrinos slip away, oh so low.
They giggle mixed up, undefined bliss,
In this microscopic, humorous abyss.

Silly puzzles that keep us awake,
In every glitch, the cosmos shakes.
Here's to the tiniest knuckleheads found,
In their wacky world, we're all spellbound.

Dimensionally Deranged

In dimensions where logic takes a break,
Time does somersaults, make no mistake.
Gravity giggles, gives a light squeeze,
Bending our minds like a soft breeze.

From the fourth dimension, a party invites,
Echoes of laughter spread through the nights.
Shapes that twist, and geometry bends,
Curved lines are paths where confusion mends.

Silly paradoxes twist and sway,
In a multi-universe, we all play.
Laughter bubbles up in every fold,
In dimensions deranged, stories unfold.

So let us ponder this cosmic mess,
Nothing is normal—and that's for the best.
In this realm of madness, let's dance and glide,
For in this chaos, our joys collide.

Breaths of the Multiverse

In the cosmos, cats may chill,
Purring softly, bending will.
Frogs in space can leap and hop,
While wishing stars just never stop.

Planets dance in tangled shoes,
Sorting socks in vibrant hues.
Galaxies share a cheeky wink,
As time flows faster than we blink.

Coffee brews in quantum ways,
Creating dreams of brighter days.
Each sip a jump across the years,
With laughter echoing through cheers.

Reality's a funny jest,
A game of luck in cosmic vest.
With every tick, we giggle loud,
In this odd, enchanted crowd.

Fragments of a Timeless Tapestry

Threads of fate, all woven tight,
Stitching moments, day and night.
A tapestry of silly lines,
Where laughter dances, and joy shines.

Each knot a story, snugly wrapped,
Where time is lost but never trapped.
Jokes arise from threads misplaced,
In this design, we're all embraced.

Tangled yarn in colors bright,
We spin our tales with pure delight.
Fingers meet in playful spins,
Where every end just speaks of wins.

In this fabric, quirks arise,
Stitching giggles, oh so sly.
As we unravel side by side,
Infinite threads in joy abide.

Schrödinger's Paradox of Poetry

A cat's both here and there, you see,
In a box of mystery, full of glee.
As words collide in playful space,
Hilarity's drawn, a funny face.

With lines that dance in odd routines,
And paradoxes in between.
Is the punchline real or fake?
We giggle hard, make no mistake.

Two truths collide in cosmic jest,
The best of both, a clever test.
Each stanza winks, alive, confused,
In a world where rhyme is amused.

Poems play by different rules,
Breaking norms, like silly fools.
In this strange realm where laughter's king,
Nonsense reigns, and joy takes wing.

The Rhythm of Quantum Moments

Time ticks on, a lively beat,
Moments swirl like dancing feet.
Each second hops, a merry tune,
As laughter lifts beneath the moon.

Every tick brings a fresh surprise,
Subatomic joys that mesmerize.
A syncopation of the mind,
Where wit and whimsy intertwine.

Particles in playful sway,
Create a rhythm, bright and gray.
Each heartbeat echoes, loud and proud,
In this charade of joy, we're cowed.

Step in sync with all that gleams,
And laugh along with wild dreams.
For in this dance, we find our place,
In quantum fun with laughter's grace.

Ripples Through the Void

In a universe so vast, we jest,
Each particle's a clown at best.
They dance in paths we can't quite trace,
Creating giggles in empty space.

Is it the quark or the leptons' play?
Making chaos their main buffet.
With every blink, they change their role,
Who knew physics could tickle the soul?

Spin me round, let's take a chance,
Entangled minds, a cosmic dance.
Surely, here, we'll find a spark,
Or just a quip in the dark.

Jokes collide like stars so bright,
In the physics of pure delight.
So laugh along, let troubles flee,
For laughter's the true mystery.

The Poetry of Potentiality

In a state, where jokes are stored,
The cosmos waits to be adored.
With each wave, a pun may bloom,
In regions vast, where laughter zooms.

Like Schrödinger's cat with a twist,
Both alive and dead, it insists.
Is it a joke or serious cheer?
Depends if someone's really here!

Behold potential in every grin,
New realities where laughs begin.
Flip a coin, it's bound to be,
A side for you, a side for me!

From coiled strings to echoes bright,
These whimsical worlds, a pure delight.
So ponder deep, but don't forget,
A giggle's truth is the best bet.

Adventures Beyond the Observable

Oh, the things that lurk outside,
Where logic and fun collide.
Through telescopes, we scan the night,
But who needs sight to feel the light?

Perhaps a star has whispered cheer,
Making cosmic jokes we cannot hear.
For in the void, a punchline flies,
And laughter echoes in the skies.

Warped timelines twist and turn,
As we ponder what we yearn.
In unreal realms, let's take a leap,
Into the jokes that made us weep.

For humor lives in every place,
Even in dark's deep embrace.
So welcome all, both far and near,
For laughter's the best souvenir!

Fractals of Fantasy

In a pattern where humor bends,
Laughter loops and never ends.
Each giggle sprouts like branches wide,
In fractals, joy cannot hide.

Zoom in close, see jesting grace,
In every corner, a friendly face.
A silly riddle, a comic pun,
In infinite layers, the fun's just begun.

Like fractals, jokes repeat and flow,
In ever smaller, a grander show.
Each echoing laugh, a soft embrace,
In a quantum world, where smiles take place.

So dance along this merry trend,
Where every joke invites a friend.
In a universe designed for cheer,
The fractals of fun are always near!

Lightyear Lullabies

In a space where giggles fly,
Stars dance on a trampoline sky.
Light beams twinkle, can't you see?
A cosmic joke just made for me.

With laughter echoing through the void,
Galactic clowns have all deployed.
Nebulas wear their finest suits,
Joking with comets, sharing roots.

Silhouettes of Schrödinger's Cat

In the box, what's inside?
A purring furball, or might it hide?
A riddle wrapped in a furry coat,
Both snoozing and plotting, a clever goat.

Paws that dance in a quantum fog,
Is it a cat, or just a smog?
Schrödinger chuckles, can't you tell?
His feline friend knows all too well.

Whims of the Universe

The universe plays its tricks on us,
With playful stars, a cosmic bus.
Gravity's giggles, black holes grin,
Spinning around, let the fun begin.

Planets dash in a wild parade,
Chasing laughter, never afraid.
Colors collide in a wobbly dance,
Caught in the whims of a serendipitous chance.

Fleeting Moments

Time ticks by in a cheeky way,
Moments slip through like children at play.
A blink, a laugh, a pop of a star,
Each tick a giggle, oh, how bizarre!

Snapshots of joy, framed in a glance,
Each fleeting tick gets its chance.
Caught in a bubble, then it's gone,
But who needs moments? Let's just move on!

Lasting Waves

Waves of laughter crash on the shore,
Jokes in tides, who could ask for more?
In every splash, a pun takes flight,
The ocean giggles, both day and night.

Rolling and tumbling, a wave of cheer,
Echoing joy, it's perfectly clear.
Even the seaweed joins the jest,
As laughter's ripples are truly the best.

Gravity's Gentle Laughter

Why do atoms play peek-a-boo?
They don't want to be seen, it's true!
Falling apples in glee, take a dive,
But up they go, in the cosmic jive.

Floating clowns on a trampoline,
Dance around like a silly machine.
Gravity giggles, it's all a game,
Pulling and pushing, never the same.

Fluctuations of Fanciful Futures

In a world where cats rule the day,
Fish might just start to walk and play.
Flip a coin, oh, what will it be?
A pizza slice or a cup of tea?

Future's uncertain, like socks on a chair,
Will frogs wear hats, or just float in air?
Every twist brings a new delight,
Dreams jump and dance, oh, what a sight!

The Entropy of Eloquent Echoes

Whispers of chaos, scattered around,
Echoes of laughter, so profound.
Entropy sings in a wacky tone,
Making sense of nonsense, overblown.

Each step we take, the universe sways,
In the dance of confusion, all our ways.
A spoonful of giggles, on life's grand stage,
Spinning in circles, let out a rage!

Cosmic Serendipity in Stanzas

Stars collide with a clumsy twirl,
Making wishes out of a dizzy whirl.
Galaxies grin as they cross their paths,
In the web of laughter where nothing lasts.

Planets hold parties, with comets as guests,
Joking around in their cosmic vests.
In the starlit dance of the absurd night,
Life's a joke, but oh, what a flight!

Fractal Fancies

In a universe that's oh so vast,
Patterns repeat, but jokes fade fast.
Every corner holds a twist or turn,
Just like my socks, which always churn.

Laughter spirals, a never-ending dance,
With each echo, the cosmos takes a chance.
A smile reflects in dimensions unseen,
As I trip over fractals—oh, what a scene!

The chaos giggles, it tumbles and rolls,
Mass and energy, or just playful trolls?
In the heart of a joke, the truth gently weaves,
Tickles and tugs, like mischievous leaves.

Infinity chuckles, takes a silly leap,
Circles of humor, in cosmic keep.
From tiny quarks to galaxies wide,
Fractal fancies, with laughter, we glide.

The Humor of Heisenberg

Heisenberg said, uncertainty reigns,
Like my thoughts on Mondays, it's always in chains.
If I know just where my keys might go,
It's guaranteed they'll be lost, that I know!

In this world of particles and speed,
One minute I'm certain, the next a bit freed.
Jokes dance around, in and out of sight,
Like photons in shadows, they bring sheer delight.

A laugh can be here, then vanish away,
Just like my luck on a rainy day.
What's funny today may not be tomorrow,
As I question the fridge—do I emit sorrow?

In the realm of quips, I shall take a stance,
With laughter so bright, let's join the dance!
Though uncertainty's here, let's not lose our grip,
For the humor of life is a magical trip.

Playful Paradoxes

A cat in a box, oh what a tale,
It's both here and there, oh how it prevails!
The paradox giggles, in shadows it plays,
As I question my snacks, in silly arrays.

Jokes twist and turn, like Schrödinger's fate,
Both silly and serious, a wobbly state.
A laugh may be heavy, yet light as a feather,
In this quirky cosmos, all drift together.

Suspend your disbelief, let humor unfold,
With riddles that shimmer, and stories retold.
In realms of mirth, every truth seems to bend,
Where every punchline can be a friend.

So flip through the verses, enjoy the charade,
With quirky confusions that never do fade.
In playful paradox, our laughter ignites,
As we dance with the cosmos on starlit nights.

The Laughter Between Worlds

Between the worlds where humor plays,
Laughter is currency, in joyous arrays.
A tickle of wit, across dimensions wide,
Together we chortle, with glee we collide.

Through wormholes of whimsy, we bounce and twirl,
In multiverse madness, our giggles unfurl.
What's serious here may just be a jest,
In the heart of chaos, we find our best.

As particles spin and realities blend,
The jokes cross the void, on which we depend.
Between every heartbeat, a punchline may leap,
In the laughter between worlds, there's magic to keep.

So let's raise a cheer to the cosmic surprise,
Where humor connects us, under vast skies.
In this tapestry woven with laughter and light,
Together we revel in the joy of night.

Love in a Binary Universe

We fell in code, two bits entwined,
In a web of zeros, our hearts aligned.
Data packets sent with endless cheer,
A glitch of passion, oh my dear!

Our love a function, so hard to trace,
Error 404 in the cosmic space.
Yet every heartbeat streams with flair,
A binary blaze in the digital air!

Is it love or just an upgrade spree?
Debugging feelings, let's wait and see.
In this matrix, we're one of a kind,
Two souls in sync, perfectly designed.

So let's compile joy, free from delay,
In a binary universe, we'll dance and sway.
In every loop, let laughter expand,
Together in bits, forever hand in hand.

Verses in Flux

Life's a wave, a bouncing sphere,
One moment one, the next we cheer.
Patterns twist with a comical flair,
As we ride the currents, without a care.

Chaos reigns in our playful minds,
Spinning jokes that tickle and bind.
In every flux, humor takes flight,
A dance of words in the dim twilight.

We drift on whims like particles free,
With quips that spark like energy.
Between the beats of laughter's beat,
Our quirky rhymes make time skip a beat.

So grab a friend, let's bridge the divide,
In the shifts of time, let joy be our guide.
In this cosmic farce, let's play our part,
With verses in flux, and an open heart!

Tidal Echoes of Existence

Riding the waves, I hear the call,
The tides of life, we laugh and fall.
In the swell of mirth, we find our place,
Echoes of joy in this endless race.

The ocean's humor splashes around,
With every wave, a new chuckle found.
From shore to shore, laughter's embrace,
A ripple of smiles we all can trace.

Jokes like surfboards crash and glide,
On shores of time, we take the ride.
With every swell, hearts open wide,
In tidal echoes, our quirks collide.

So let the waves wash worries away,
With laughter's tide, we'll play all day.
In this ocean of cosmic jest,
With humor's splash, we're truly blessed!

Quirks of the Cosmos

In cosmic corners, where stars collide,
Galactic giggles and lunar pride.
From black holes' chuckles to comets' grins,
The universe laughs, where all begins.

In space's quirk, where oddities bloom,
A dance of atoms in starlit rooms.
Supernovae wink like playful clowns,
While the Milky Way spins and spins around.

Time ticks funny, bending with glee,
A punchline woven in the fabric we see.
With every quirk, a chuckle escapes,
In the grand design, we make our shapes.

So raise a toast to the stellar spree,
In quirks of cosmos, we're wild and free.
From cosmic balance to whimsical play,
Laughter's the light that shows us the way!

The Silence Between Frequencies

In a world of waves that bounce and play,
The silence dances, oh what a display!
Bantering particles have much to share,
But whispering photons float light as air.

Entangled jokes make us scratch our heads,
While electrons giggle in their fast treads.
Wondering if they'll ever collide,
As the universe chuckles, we can't hide.

Momentum's got a sense of delight,
In every slip and slide through the night.
Witty quarks bounce off the cosmic wall,
Competing for laughs, they bob and sprawl.

With every pulse, a punchline is found,
As laughter ripples through the vast ground.
The silence humors the broad expanse,
In a game where logic and laughter dance.

Cosmic Contradictions in Couplets

Stars twinkle, yet they're quite far away,
Like a shy friend hiding on a playday.
Gravity's grip pulls you to the ground,
While floating thoughts are so joyfully unbound.

The faster you go, the slower the clock,
With time's antics, we just gawk and mock.
Waves in suits dancing side by side,
Yet when one dips, the other's wide-eyed.

Protons joke with a neutron's frown,
In the nucleus of humor, they clown around.
Entangled like a tangled set of threads,
Familiar faces from the particles' heads.

Thus, in this cosmic comedy we dwell,
With laughs that echo like a purring bell.
In contradiction, we find our delight,
As the universe knows how to laugh at the night.

Laughter in Lightyears

Across the vastness, a giggle does roam,
A comet's tail tickles the cold dark dome.
Stars share stories in sparkles and light,
While planets roll over in playful plight.

Supernovae burst into fits of glee,
While black holes munch snacks—so carefree!
Each lightyear traveled with a chuckle or two,
Finding the humor in the cosmic view.

Pulsars spin tales that make the void laugh,
In a cosmic bar, they share a good chaff.
Time may be funny, or maybe it's just me,
In the realm of existence, it's glee we see.

So here we float, on this laugh-filled ride,
With stars as our guides, and humor as our pride.
Through galaxies swirling, we find our cheer,
For laughter in lightyears is ever so near.

Reflections of a Photon's Journey

A photon sets off on a whim to explore,
Reflecting on nothing, but wanting much more.
It bounces through mirrors with cheeky delight,
Inverting its path, what a curious sight!

In every encounter, there's mischief to share,
As it flits past starlight, without a care.
"Why do I shimmer?" it jests with a grin,
"Because I'm no particle, I'm all about spin!"

It prances through prisms, in colors so bright,
Creating rainbows, oh what a flight!
"Catch me if you can!" it shouts with a laugh,
While waves in synchrony share in its path.

But when it comes home, the cosmos will see,
The laughter of light is a grand jubilee.
For every reflection holds stories untold,
In the journey of photons, their humor unfolds.

Lighthearted Loops

In a universe of bends and jives,
The particles dance, oh how they strive.
They swirl like dancers on a stage,
In a cosmic ball, they engage.

A photon jumps, takes a twirl,
It zips past electrons in a whirl.
With a wink and a giggle, it plays tag,
While neutrinos slip through, never lag.

Time loops in circles, a dizzy spree,
Making sure nothing's as it seems to be.
With laughter echoing through the void,
We embrace the chaos, unannoyed.

So when you think of serious space,
Remember the glee in its vast embrace.
For even in shadows where mysteries glue,
There's humor aplenty for me and you.

The Playful Particle

A boson bounced with boundless cheer,
It tickled photons, oh so near.
In a realm where jokes grow tall,
Every quark held the laughter's call.

Protons giggled, and neutrons snickered,
In the dance of atoms, joy flickered.
With every reaction, a funny twist,
In the game of science, who could resist?

The smallest bits were jolly, bright,
Creating energy with pure delight.
While electrons sparked a disco ball,
In the particle party, we had a ball!

So send a wink to those tiny friends,
Their funny antics never end.
In the vast expanse, don't take a sigh,
For even particles love to fly high!

Gravity's Chuckle

Oh gravity, you thief of fun,
You pull us down, but don't outrun.
With a belly laugh, you hug the ground,
In your arms, those giggles abound.

Can't escape your playful grip,
As we stumble, tumble, and trip.
You say, 'Stay close, don't get too free,'
While we headbutt the floor in glee.

Planets whirl in your funny game,
Spinning like tops, they feel no shame.
In a cosmic joke, we find our peace,
For every footer felt, there's joy's release.

So here's to you, oh tricky force,
We laugh as we follow your course.
For in your pull, the world spins round,
With witty wonders, joy is found.

Superposition of Silly

In a world of choices, so many to see,
Superpositions giggle just like me.
Am I here? Or maybe there?
In a tangle of options, what do I wear?

Cats that are both, alive and not,
Twirling in boxes, they give quite a shot.
With a wink, they smile, in a clever chase,
Defying logic with each playful space.

When outcomes collide, it's truly a blast,
Every possibility, a joy unsurpassed.
So when you're uncertain, just take a leap,
In the realm of the silly, dive in deep!

Oh, the laughter that ripples through time,
It shimmers like stars, in rhythm and rhyme.
With every laugh, a wave is made,
In the dance of the cosmos, we gladly wade!

Entangled Verses

In a world where particles dance,
Two photons share a quirky chance.
They giggle and they sway around,
In a game of hide and seek, they've found.

They wink and nod from far apart,
It's a cosmic joke, an artful start.
A smile across a vast expanse,
Their connection is the craziest romance.

Infinity calls with a teasing tone,
Yet here we are, all alone.
Stuck in traffic of the mind,
While they play tag, so unconfined.

So let's raise a toast to this strange bond,
Where no distance can leave us beyond.
With every laugh, the universe spins,
In entangled joys, where humor begins.

The Melody of Superstrings

Tickle those strings, play a sweet tune,
Bouncing through galaxies under the moon.
Grab your violin, let's catch a wave,
In this funny dance, we dare to be brave.

These tiny strings vibrate with flair,
Creating a symphony high in the air.
A high note here, a low note there,
Just don't ask the quarks, they don't play fair.

Notes twist and twirl in the cosmic night,
A melody's journey, oh what a sight!
The universe laughs, it rings and it sings,
Who knew deep thoughts could come from such things?

So dance with me in this bewildering tune,
Under bright stars and a chuckling moon.
In every frequency, laughter propels,
The strings of existence, where humor dwells.

Vibrational Verses of the Void

What echoes in the empty space?
A cosmic giggle in a timeless race.
Missing socks in a punctured sky,
Floating away as if they can fly.

The void is strange, but what a sight,
With whispers and chuckles, it takes flight.
In every quark's kaleidoscope twist,
Lies a punchline that can't be missed.

Waves crashing silently, don't be shy,
They wave at us as they pass by.
In every void, a spark of glee,
A universe built on whimsical spree.

So join the dance in this funny expanse,
Laugh with the stars in the cosmic dance.
For in the silence where echoes collide,
We find the jokes in the cosmic tide.

Thoughts Beyond the Event Horizon

What lies beyond that curious line?
A riddle wrapped in a joke divine.
Gravity's grip, a tickling bind,
While spacetime giggles, endlessly unwind.

In the depths where the light's in flight,
Thoughts spiral in with pure delight.
What's that they say? 'No way out!' they chuckle,
Even black holes have a funny knuckle.

So let's step boldly beyond that gate,
To tickle the cosmos and contemplate.
For in the depths of that swirling abyss,
Lurks the punchline we surely can't miss.

With a wink at the galaxies spinning around,
Laughter echoes where logic is drowned.
In mysterious realms, we lose our way,
Yet find joy in the universe's play.

The Lightness of Superposition

In a state of perhaps and may,
Cats chase their tails in a quantum ballet.
Two places at once, oh what a ride,
A wave of confusion, let's enjoy the tide.

Schrödinger's cat takes a nap all day,
Is it alive or just wanting to play?
With a flick of a tail, it's here then it's gone,
Living the dream while we ponder the con.

Atoms dance in undefined threads,
While we argue what's real in our beds.
In a tangle of choices, who's making the call?
Laughing at logic, we try not to fall.

In a universe where nothing is clear,
We find that absurdity gives us a cheer.
So embrace the unknown, let it all flow,
In the lightness of being, just enjoy the show.

Winks of the Cosmic Mind

The universe chuckles as it spins through space,
With comets that wink, oh the wonders we chase.
Stars giggle in clusters, a celestial tease,
While planets exchange their own cosmic wheeze.

A black hole grins slyly, 'Come closer, my dear!'
But you'd better hold on, it's a wild frontier.
Particles frolic in a vibrant array,
Making jokes in a dance that we can't convey.

Galaxies swirl in a grand cosmic jest,
While skeptics insist they know what's best.
But even the wisest can slip on a quark,
Finding humor in error, igniting a spark.

So revel in laughter, it echoes through time,
In the rhythm of laughter, we find our prime.
With winks from the cosmos, we giggle and cheer,
In this vast, infinite, wondrous frontier.

Curved Paths of Curiosity

In the twist of a proton, there's boundless delight,
As we wander through realms both baffling and bright.
Curved paths we follow, on whims we embark,
Each loop a new riddle, each glance leaves a mark.

With curiosity piqued, we ask, what's the joke?
The universe giggles, oh what a stroke!
Entangled and baffled, we run in a race,
Chasing the laughter that dances in space.

Light bends and it giggles, not straight as we thought,
In dimensions of silliness, knowledge is caught.
We prowl through the cosmos, with questions in tow,
Finding smiles in puzzles, what fun do we sow!

So follow the curves and embrace each new twist,
In the laughter of science, we cannot resist.
With each little wonder, let wonderment start,
In the dance of discovery, let joy be our art.

Beneath the Wavefunction's Veil

Under the veil where mysteries lie,
Reality flirts with a winking eye.
The wavefunction twirls, a mischievous sprite,
In shadows of truth, it has its own light.

Particles giggle, as if in a play,
Choosing their paths in a whimsical way.
Oft lost in the shuffle, yet never alone,
In the pulse of the moment, oddities are sown.

With each wave that dances and bends in the night,
Giggles of physics make everything right.
The veil parts just slightly, a chuckle comes through,
As hilarity blooms in the fabric we knew.

So peek behind curtains, let laughter prevail,
In the whims of the cosmos, we set sail.
For beneath the sweet veil of what we can measure,
Lives laughter in paradox, a cosmic treasure.

The Symphony of Subatomic Silence

In tiny realms where particles play,
A whisper of chaos rules the day.
Electrons jiggle, protons spin,
While neutrinos sneak out, just to grin.

Waves collide in a feather-light fray,
For every photon that comes to sway.
Antimatter's cousin, a cheeky ghost,
In this quirky dance, we laugh the most.

These quirks and jests make atoms sing,
A comic ballet, a subatomic fling.
With each quark's giggle, gravity bends,
Creating wonders that never end.

So tip your hat to the unseen jest,
In this silent symphony, we are blessed.
With laughter echoing through the void,
In every quark, joy is deployed.

Poems from the Eventual Horizon

At the edge of a black hole's grin,
Matter braves a wild spin.
Falling in, they shout with glee,
'Guess it's time for a cosmic spree!'

Time wobbles, like a jelly on a plate,
As light appears to dance with fate.
Photons pirouette, then take a dive,
As laughter echoes, feeling alive.

Gravity pulls with a playful tug,
While space-time wraps around like a hug.
If you're lost and can't find your way,
Just join the party; it's quite a ballet!

So gaze into the night's twinkling eye,
And hear the universe chuckle, oh my!
With jokes so vast, they bend the light,
At the horizon, every laugh's a delight.

Stanzas in a Cosmic Dance

Stars waltz with planets in radiant rings,
While moons tap their toes to the cosmic strings.
Galaxies twirl in a swirling embrace,
As the cosmos giggles in its vast space.

A neutron star spins, just like a top,
Creating ripples that never stop.
Each comet that flies with a sparkling tail,
Is a celestial note in a galactic tale.

Light years travel with a wink and a nod,
Through the tapestry of the universe, broad.
Celestial humor, a stellar jest,
In this cosmic dance, we're truly blessed.

So join the rhythm, let stardust inspire,
In this vast playground where dreams aspire.
With every twinkle, laughter's our stance,
In the dance of the cosmos, we all prance.

The Muse in Microcosms

Within tiny realms of the unseen street,
Where atoms embrace in a playful feat.
A muse of mischief whispers and shares,
The secrets of quarks with wild, frizzy hairs.

Bubbles of energy giggle and glow,
In this microcosm, it's quite the show.
Protons tease neutrinos, saying, 'Hey there!'
While photons play dress-up without a care.

Each little particle knows how to jest,
In the laughter of physics, we are guests.
With quantum tricks that put on a parade,
In these minuscule worlds, jokes are made.

So cherish the quirks of the infinitesimal,
For humor resides in this grand spectacle.
In the heart of the small, where oddities loom,
We find joy sprouting like a wild bloom.

Fuzzy Logic Fables

In a world of blurs and shades,
Doubt's a friend that often fades.
Cats and hats are quite the pair,
Yet they vanish in thin air.

When you think you're right on track,
Logic gives a gentle whack.
Ask the cat which way to go,
It grins and leaps, steals the show.

Truth's a slippery, fun-filled game,
Like a fish that slips your name.
What's real here is just a joke,
In the fog, we laugh and poke.

So embrace the fuzzy lines,
Wit and giggles intertwine.
In this realm of laugh and cheer,
Clearer thoughts will reappear.

Parallel Playfulness

Two lines that never share a meet,
Chase the laughter on repeat.
One says yes, the other no,
Together they put on a show.

In this space where echoes blend,
Strange equations often bend.
Like two clowns on a mirrored stage,
Out of sync, they still engage.

Caught between the smiles and frowns,
Making worlds where joy abounds.
Every joke is just a twist,
In this game, you can't resist.

From the sidelines, watch them play,
Every quip a bright array.
In dimensions, sly and slick,
Laughter's what we choose to pick.

Uncertainty Principle Puns

In the realm of laugh and chase,
Need a compass or a brace.
Which direction does it lean?
Funny faces, sights unseen.

One day here, the next in doubt,
Wonders twist and turn about.
You can't know just what you'll find,
But the giggles ease your mind.

Measure time, or skip a beat,
Who can tell which feels more sweet?
Schrodinger's cat plays a game,
Hiding here, but not the same.

So embrace what's lost and found,
In this puzzle, humor's crowned.
Through uncertainty, we will run,
Every slip's a spark of fun.

The Dance of Entangled Minds

When thoughts collide like stars at night,
A whirl of laughs takes off in flight.
Two minds twist, they spin and twirl,
In this dance, bright chaos whirl.

What's yours is mine, and yet it's not,
Tangled paths in playful thought.
Like dancers caught in laughter's flow,
Witty steps steal the show.

Each kick and turn absurdity finds,
As we poke at tangled binds.
Eureka moments, not so clear,
Just a chuckle or a cheer.

So grab a friend, let's shake it out,
In this dance, erase the doubt.
Entangled in the jokes we weave,
Side by side, we'll never leave.

Temporal Ticktock and Tethers

Time's a trickster, plays peekaboo,
It bounces around like it's lost its shoe.
Moments in knots, tangled with glee,
I thought I was early, but who's counting me?

Clocks giggle softly, they whisper and tease,
As seconds do somersaults with such ease.
Winding and looping, they dance in delight,
While I stand here baffled, lost in the night.

Branches of past twisting, daring their fate,
How many of me stand at the gate?
One's juggling time, while another plays chess,
Surprise, it's a party — oh, what a mess!

So here's to the tickers, that laugh as they fly,
Who'd think that moments could frolic and sigh?
In the game of existence, we're all just a bit,
With time as our jester, we're bound to submit.

The Poetry of Particle Play

Frolicking photons in races of light,
Dashing through space, oh what a sight!
Bumping and colliding, they chatter and cheer,
In this wild playground, they hold nothing dear.

Electrons are sneaky, with tricks of their own,
Jumping through levels, they giggle and moan.
They hide in the shadows, like lovers in flight,
While protons stand guard, ensuring delight.

Neutrons are neutral, quite bored of the fuss,
Rolling their eyes, they just stand and discuss.
"Why must they bounce? Can't they settle down?"
As quarks throw confetti and dance all around.

Atoms in harmony, a merriment spree,
Spinning and twirling, their dance sets them free.
In the realm of the tiny, where laughter is grand,
Who knew that existence could tickle like sand?

Expressions from the Expanse

Out there in the void, where silence can sing,
Galaxies throw parties, and planets wear bling.
Stars playing hide and seek, peeking with glee,
While comets deliver their postcards from spree.

The universe winks, with its mysteries bright,
Juggling black holes like balloons in the night.
Cosmic balloons? Oh, what a sight indeed,
As they float through the heavens, no limits, no need.

Light years apart, yet we all share a laugh,
A friendly reminder, we're all in the craft.
Nebulae shimmer, like glitter spread wide,
While supernovae giggle, bursting with pride.

So here's to the vastness, our joyous domain,
Where humor and wonder constantly reign.
In the grand expanse, oh how weird things can be,
With starlight and whimsy, we're all cosmic free!

Absurdities of Atomic Anecdotes

Once an atom wandered, feeling quite bold,
Claiming it knew all the secrets of old.
"Excuse me!" it chirped, "I've plenty to share,
Like how I split with a flair, unaware!"

In gatherings of neutrons, they laughed till they cried,
As protons proclaimed, "What a wild ride!"
But electrons just giggled, too dizzy to care,
Saying, "We're all here, but who's really aware?"

With and without, the entanglements twirl,
It's hard to stay sane in this particle swirl.
Tales of collisions and sparks in the dark,
Are mixed with the jest — oh, what a lark!

So toast to the atoms, all silly and bright,
In their microscopic world, there's humor at night.
With every reaction, they dance and they play,
Boundless absurdities, come join in the fray!

www.ingramcontent.com/pod-product-compliance
Lightning Source LLC
Chambersburg PA
CBHW071835160426
43209CB00003B/312